A 2023 CALENDAR

A Tool for ESL Teachers

CREATED BY:

LYNN RICHARDSON

12

MONTH ESL/ART
LEARNING ACTIVITIES

CONTENTS

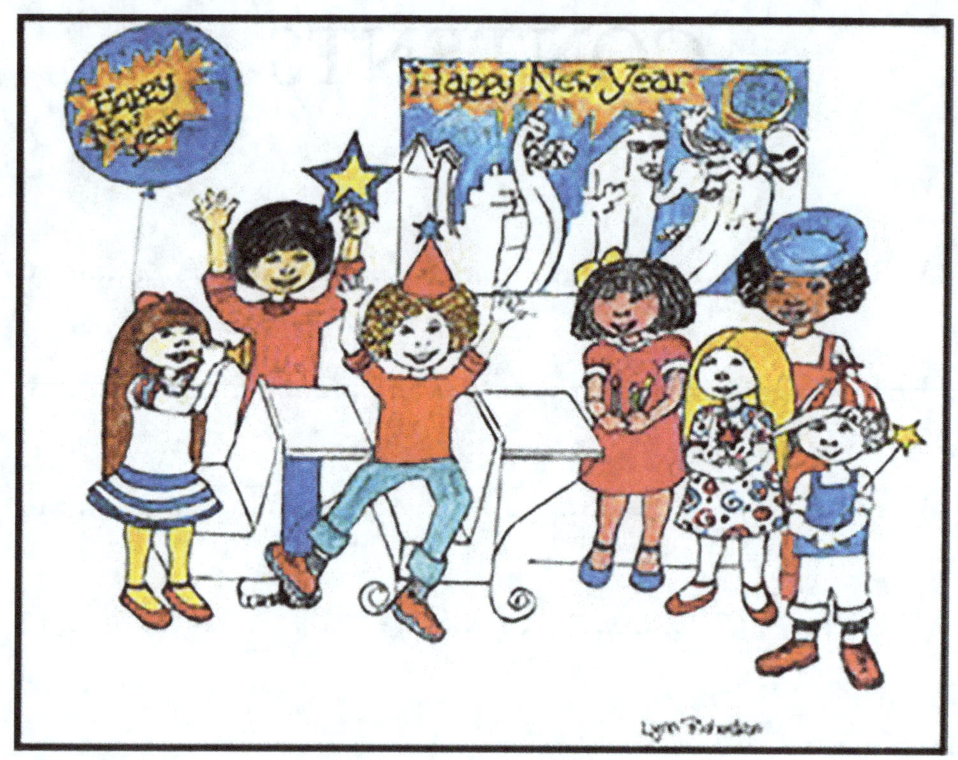

JANUARY

CELEBRATING 2023 AROUND THE WORLD

Students will share how each of them celebrated the 2023 New Year. They will explore how New Year celebrations are conducted through out the world and present their findings through visual (drawings) and oral presentations.

JANUARY A 2023 CALENDAR

SUNDAY	MONDAY	TUESDAY	WEDNESDAY	THURSDAY	FRIDAY	SATURDAY
1	2	3	4	5	6	7
8	9	10	11	12	13	14
15	16	17	18	19	20	21
22	23	24	25	26	27	28
29	30	31				

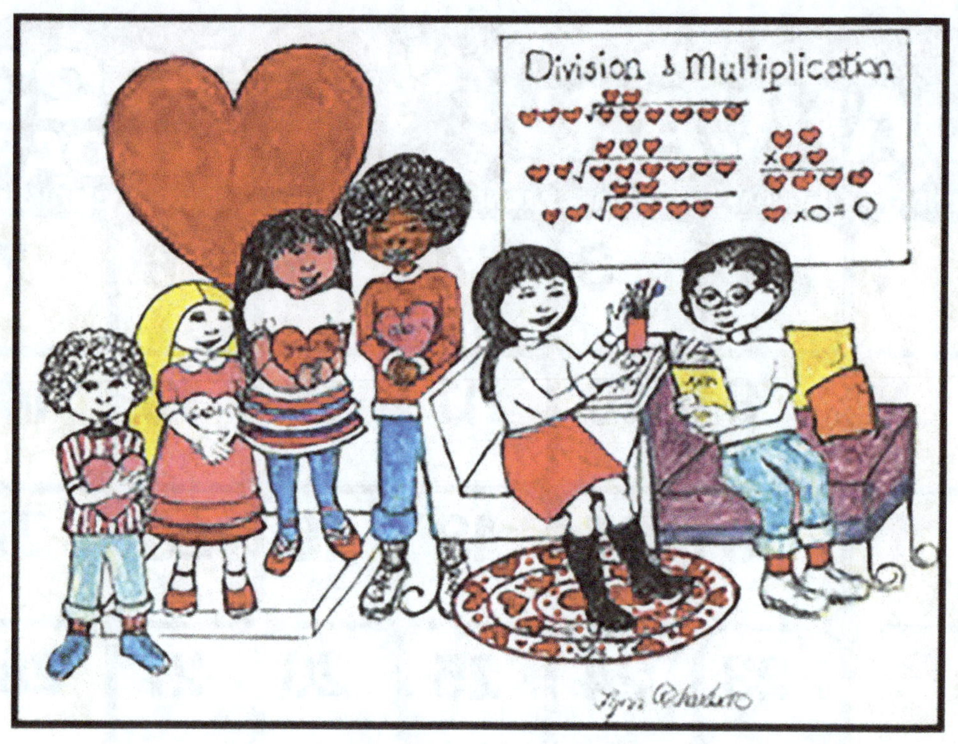

FEBRUARY

GUNG HAY FAT CHOY DESIGNS

Students learn that February is the month of love and that Feb 1 marks the Chinese New Year known as Gung Hay Fat Choy. Students will research and create lanterns, dragons, and other symbols that represent the Chinese New Year.

Students can use the valentine "hearts" themes as math counter manipulatives in across - the- curriculum division and multiplication problems and have a wonderful Valentines Day party.

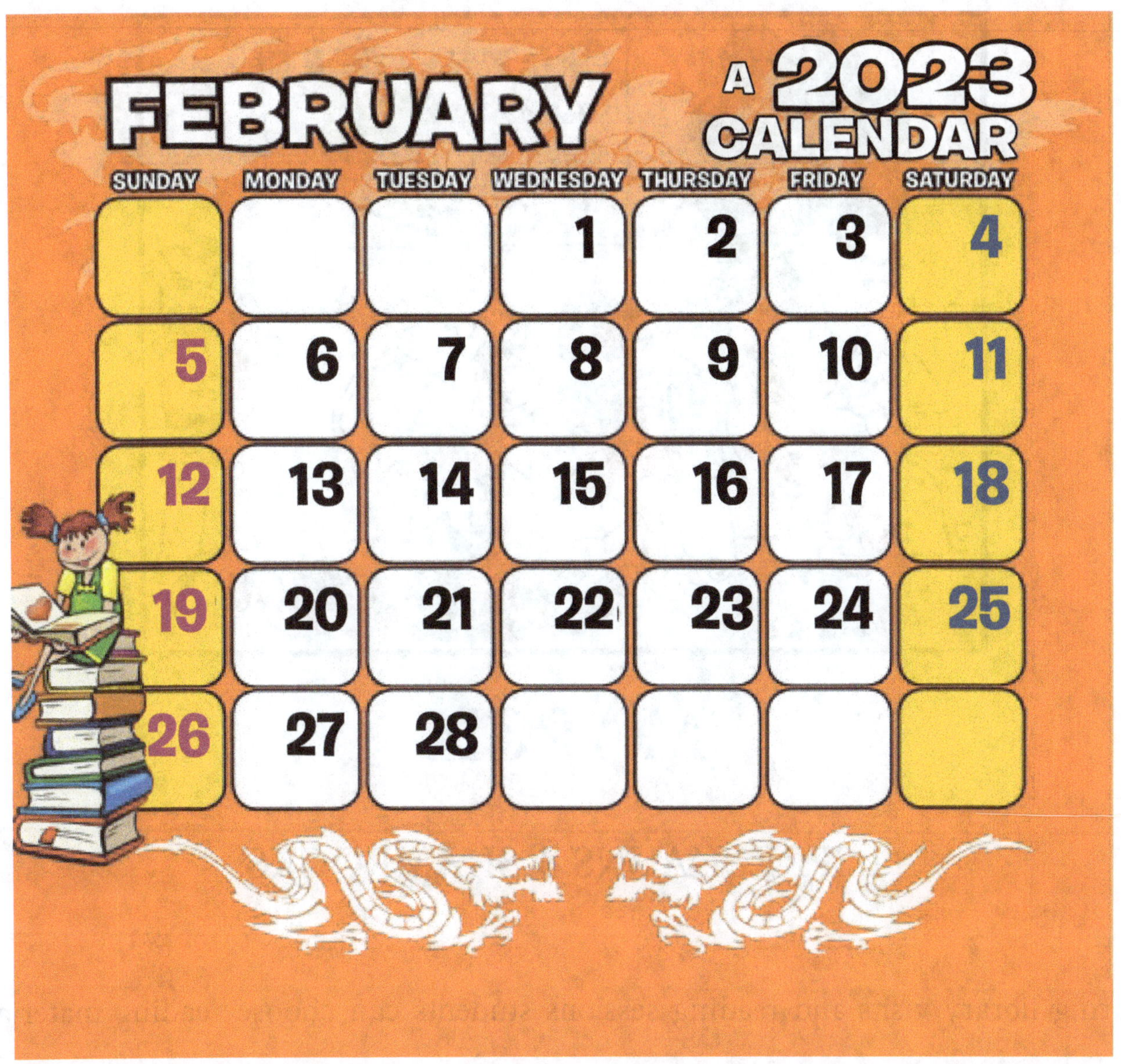

FEBRUARY
A 2023 CALENDAR
SUNDAY MONDAY TUESDAY WEDNESDAY THURSDAY FRIDAY SATURDAY
1 2 3 4
5 6 7 8 9 10 11
12 13 14 15 16 17 18
19 20 21 22 23 24 25
26 27 28

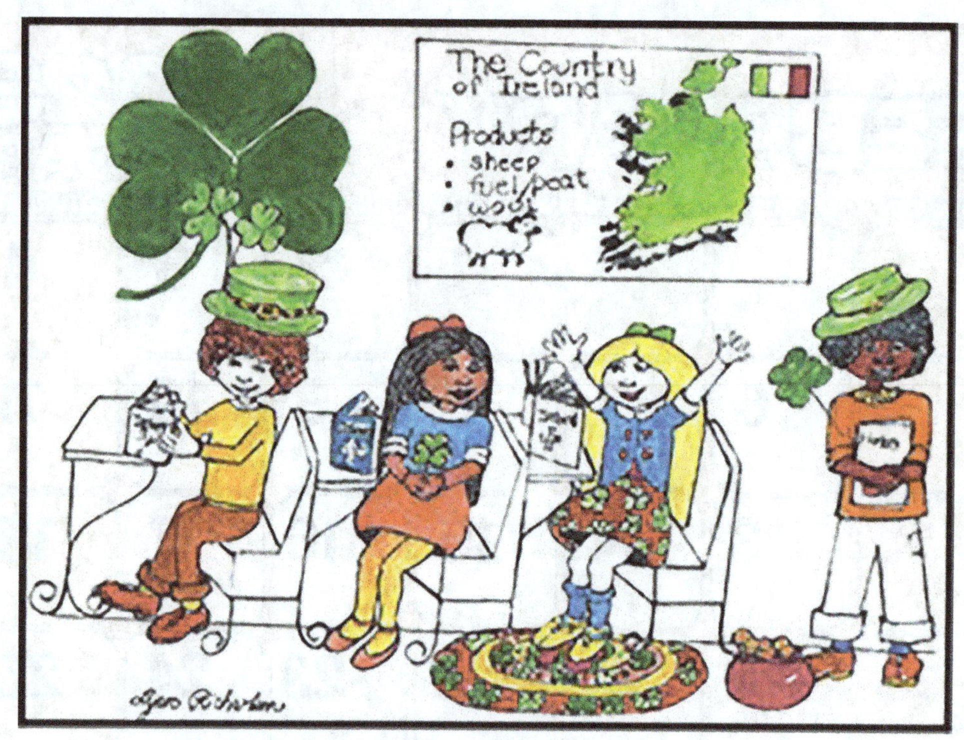

MARCH

LEPRECHAUNS & SHAMROCKS

During library visits and reading sessions students can choose reading materials about Ireland, leprechauns, and shamrocks. Following story time, students can pick related books and write short descriptive paragraphs about their favorite story. For art, students may create their own designs by tracing and drawing shamrock patterns which can be cut out and pasted underneath their written paragraphs.

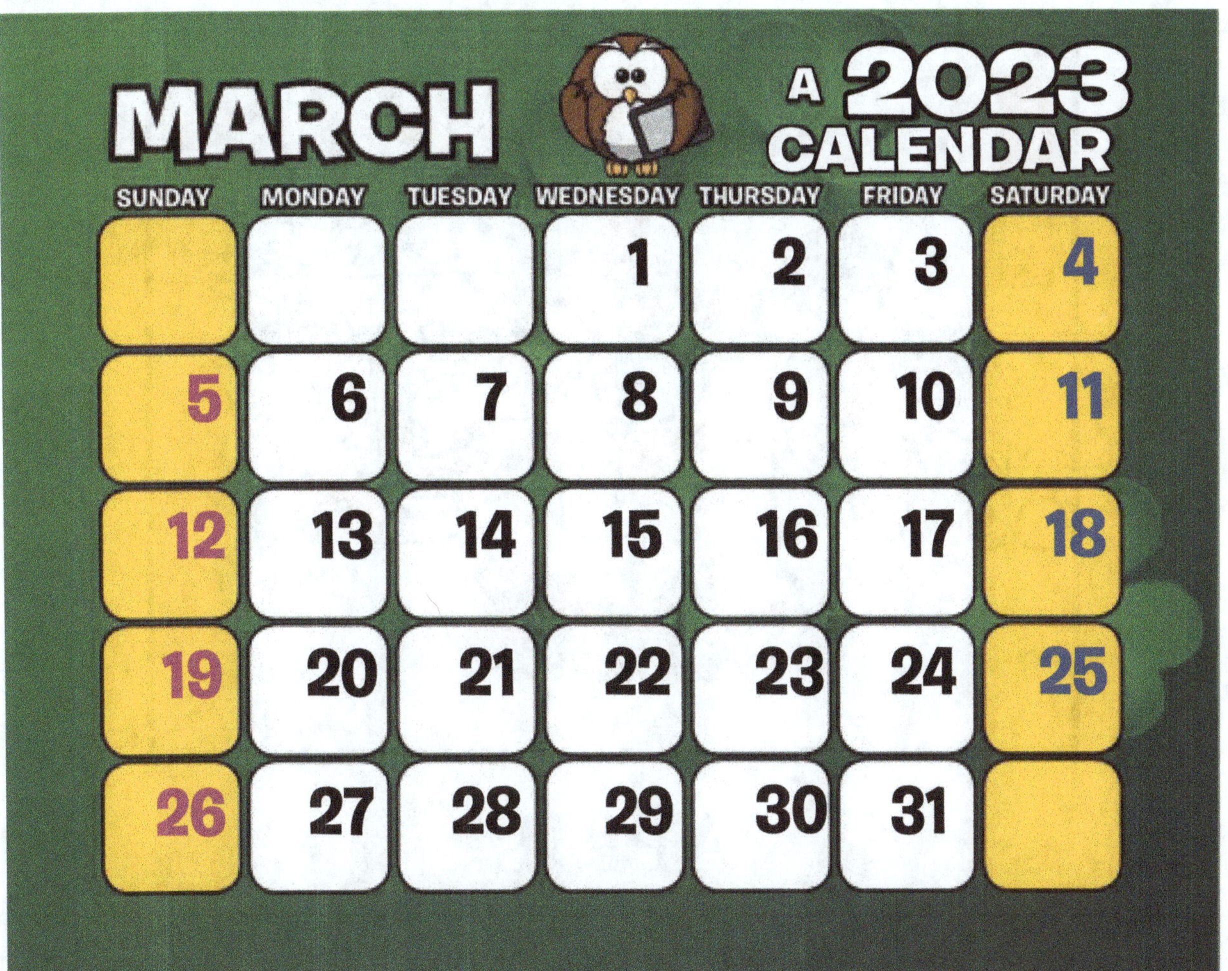

MARCH
A 2023 CALENDAR
SUNDAY MONDAY TUESDAY WEDNESDAY THURSDAY FRIDAY SATURDAY
1 2 3 4
5 6 7 8 9 10 11
12 13 14 15 16 17 18
19 20 21 22 23 24 25
26 27 28 29 30 31

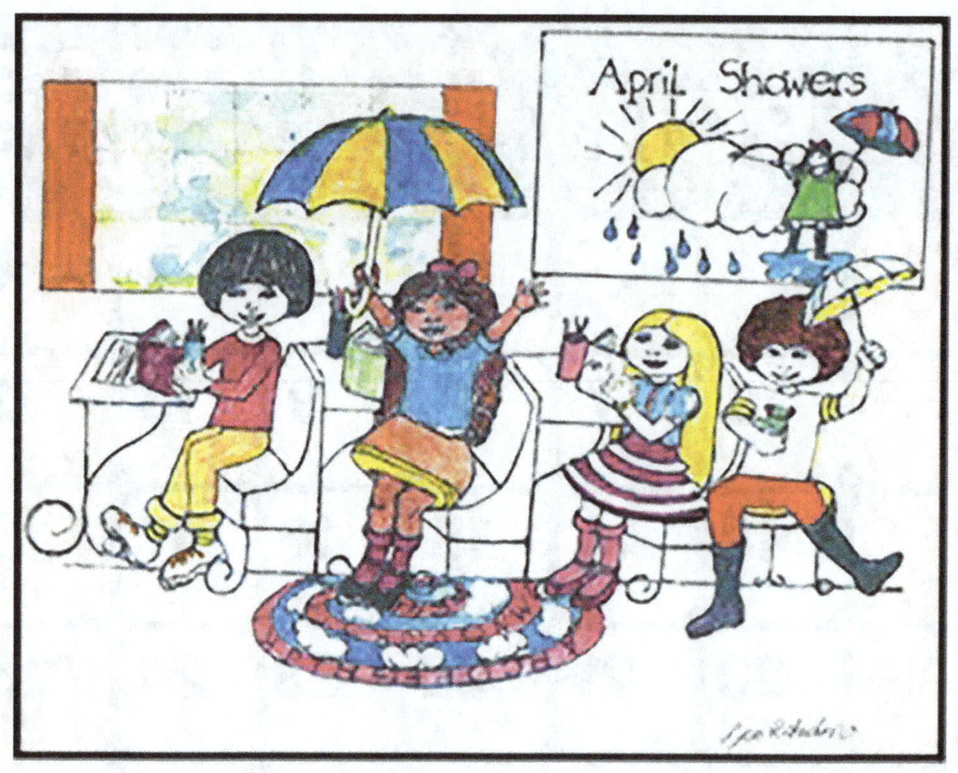

APRIL

FAVORITE CLOUD

Students will read and discover how clouds are formed and how the rain/water cycle works. Students will engage in discussions and choose what type of cloud they might be if they were a cloud and write a composition about it. For the art activity, students can draw and paint their favorite cloud or form cotton balls into their cloud shape choices, glue it, and attach it to their composition.

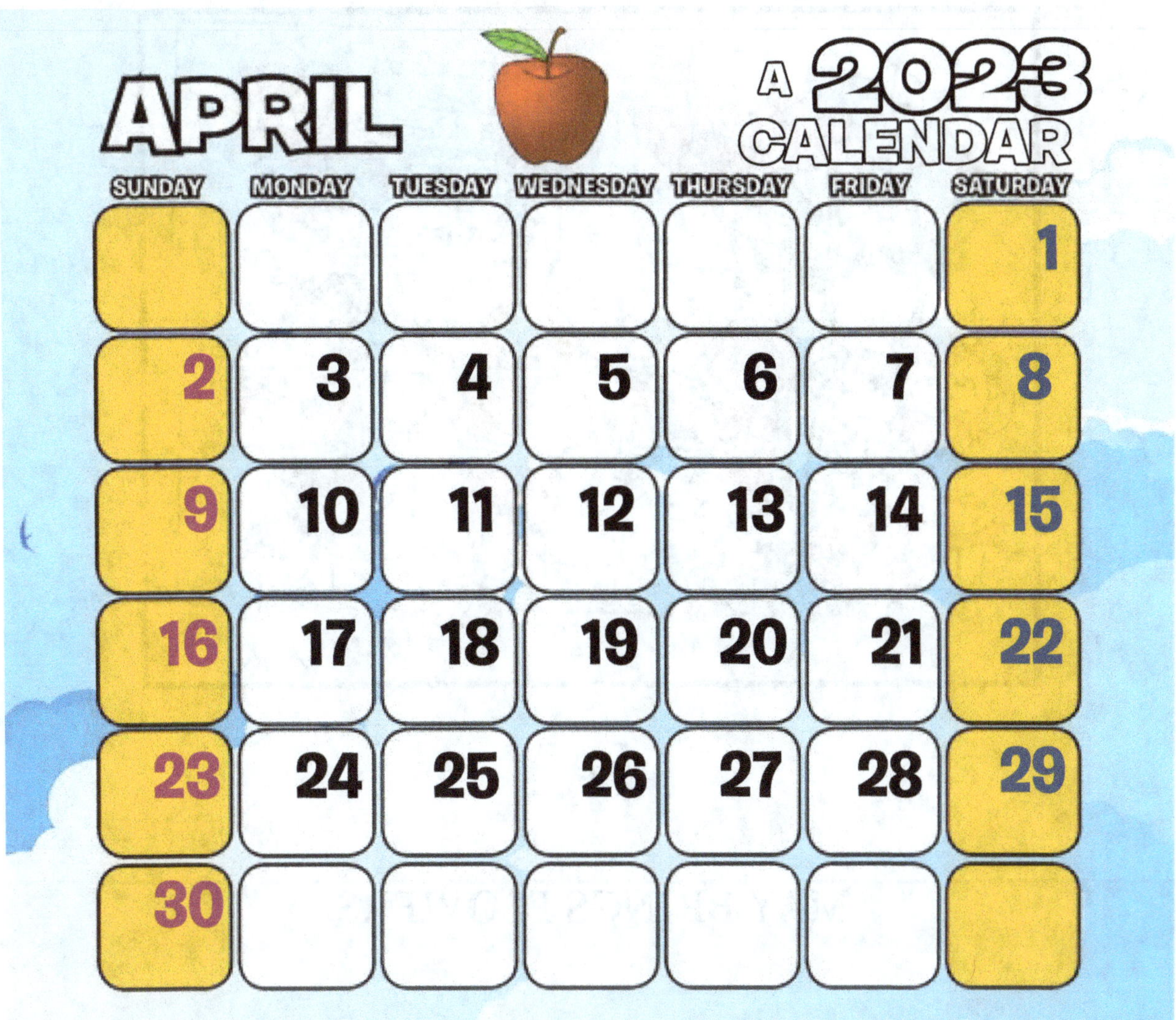

APRIL
A 2023 CALENDAR
SUNDAY MONDAY TUESDAY WEDNESDAY THURSDAY FRIDAY SATURDAY
1
2 3 4 5 6 7 8
9 10 11 12 13 14 15
16 17 18 19 20 21 22
23 24 25 26 27 28 29
30

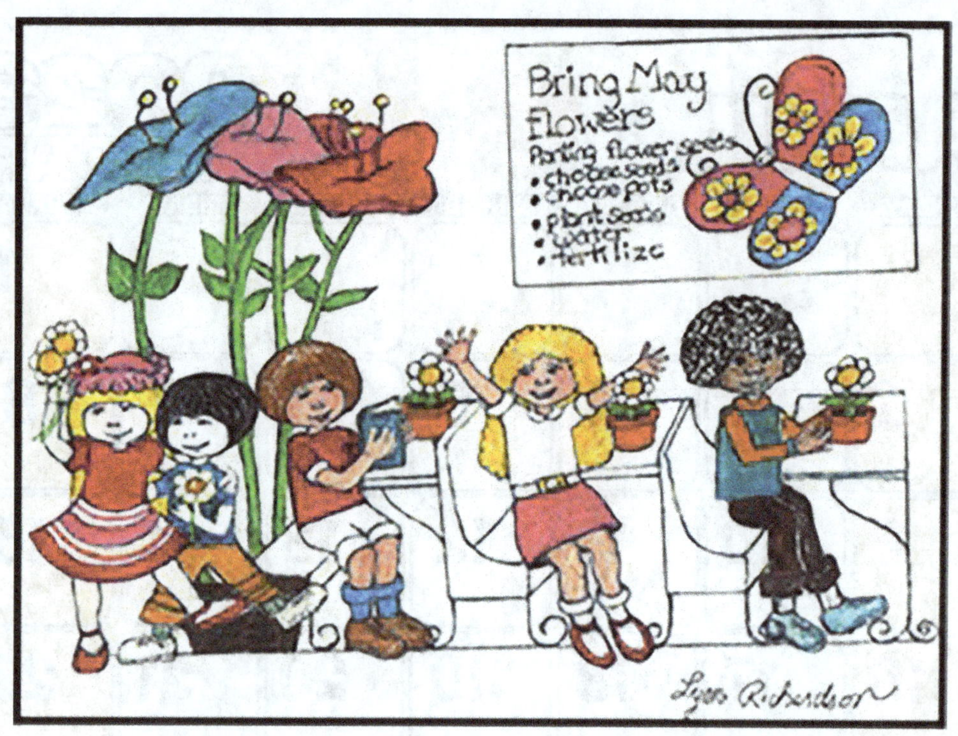

MAY

MAY BRINGS FLOWERS

Teacher gives out handouts about information on flowers and asks students to draw the parts of a flower and label them. Students will have discussions on the functions of each part. The teacher will model seed planting activities so that each student will know how to plant their flower seeds and watch them grow, grow, grow!

MAY

A 2023 CALENDAR

SUNDAY	MONDAY	TUESDAY	WEDNESDAY	THURSDAY	FRIDAY	SATURDAY
	1	2	3	4	5	6
7	8	9	10	11	12	13
14	15	16	17	18	19	20
21	22	23	24	25	26	27
28	29	30	31			

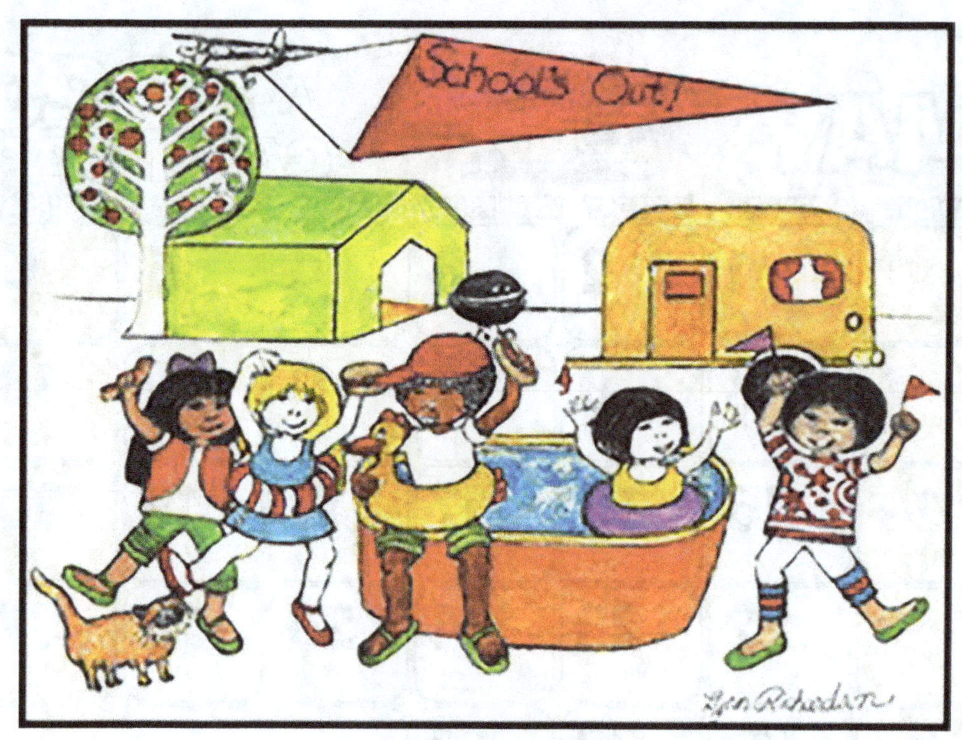

JUNE

MONARCH BUTTERFLY MIGRATION

To promote continual learning during summer break, teacher urges students to visit their public library to engage in reading programs. As an inspirational topic, students can access http://www.monarch-butterfly.com/. This will inspire students to gain information about monarch butterfly migration and help them create beautiful butterfly drawings and paintings.

JUNE

A 2023 CALENDAR
SUNDAY | MONDAY | TUESDAY | WEDNESDAY | THURSDAY | FRIDAY | SATURDAY
1 | 2 | 3
4 | 5 | 6 | 7 | 8 | 9 | 10
11 | 12 | 13 | 14 | 15 | 16 | 17
18 | 19 | 20 | 21 | 22 | 23 | 24
25 | 26 | 27 | 28 | 29 | 30

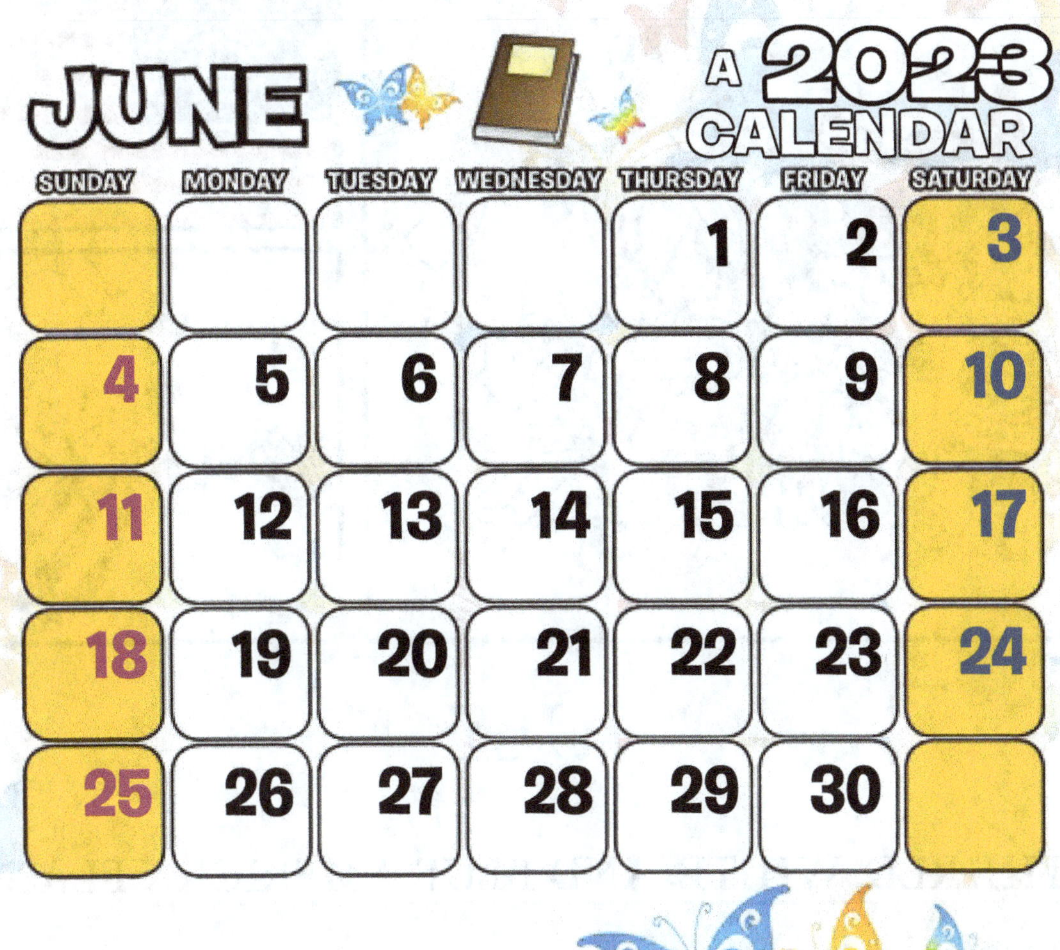

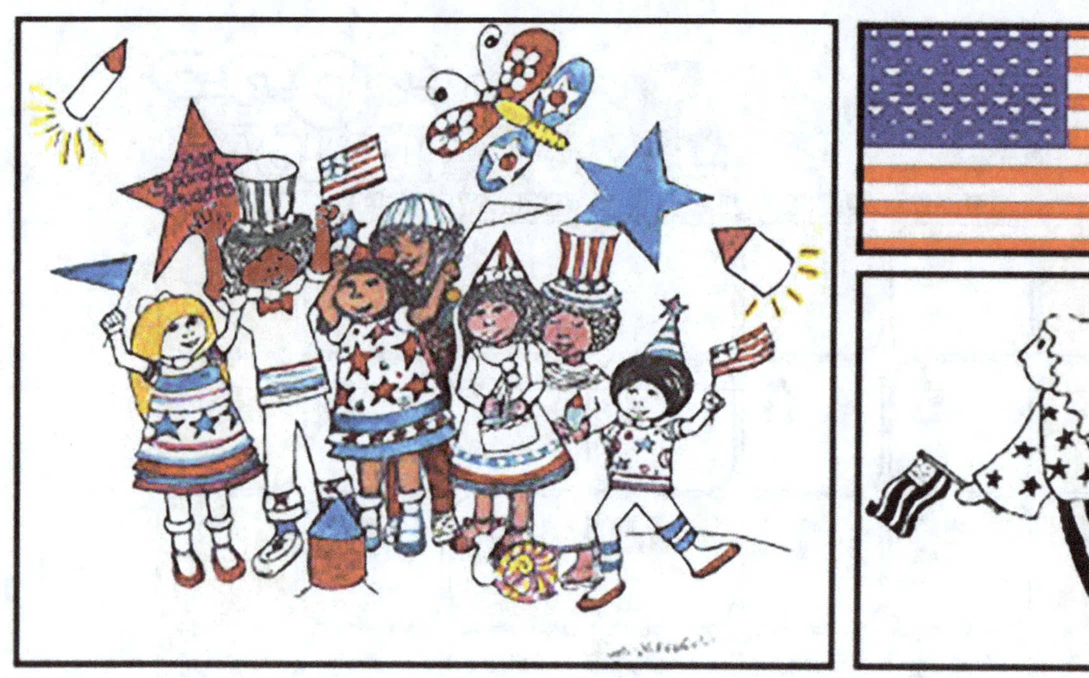

JULY

THE RED, WHITE, AND BLUE AMERICAN FLAG

Teacher will access AmericanFlag.com website for students to explore colors, concepts of freedom, and symbols that represent the meaning of freedom. After they learn what freedom means and what each color represents, they may write a descriptive sentence about what freedom means to them and color their own red, white, and blue American flag angel. (see example above)

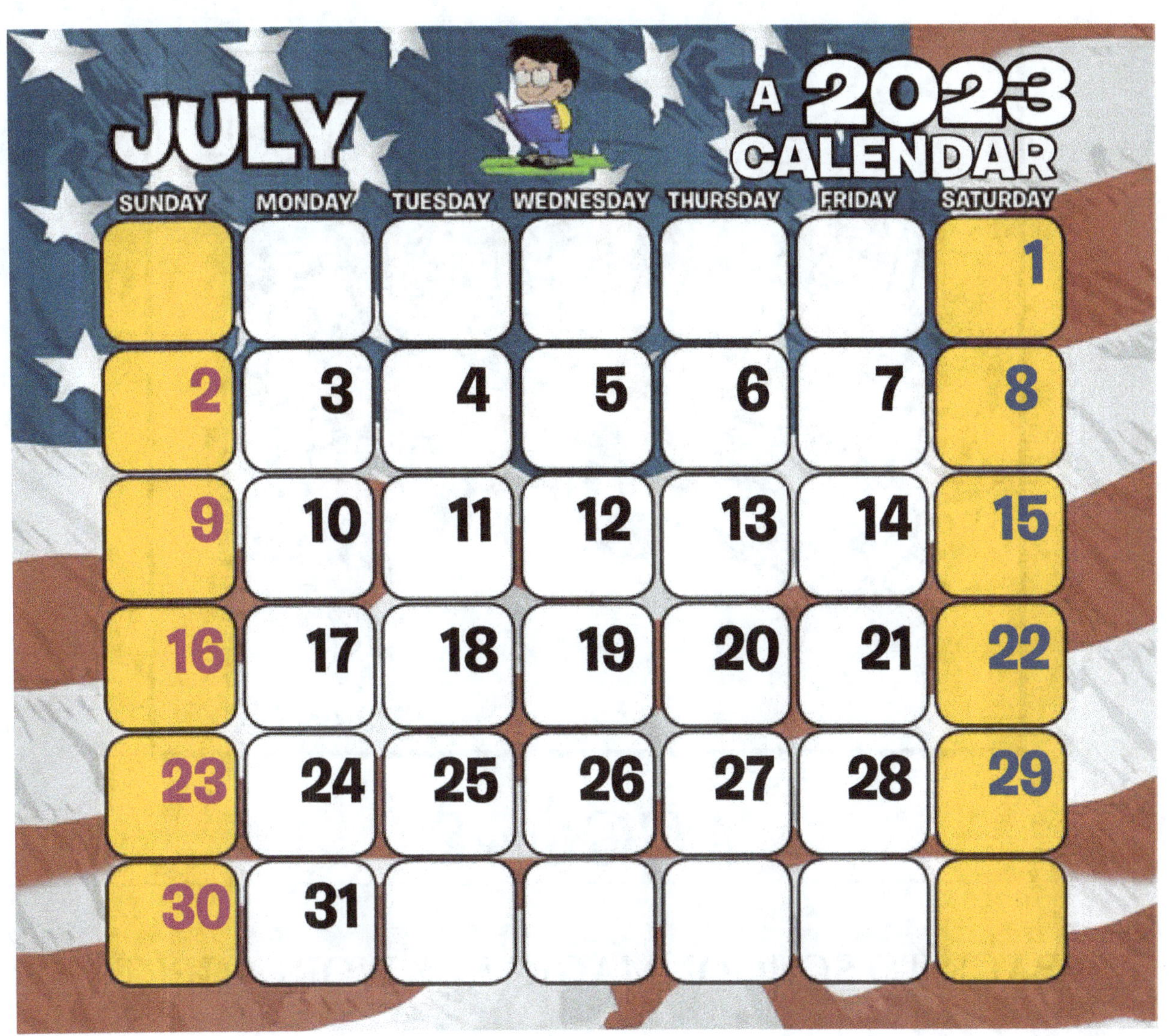

JULY
A 2023 CALENDAR
SUNDAY MONDAY TUESDAY WEDNESDAY THURSDAY FRIDAY SATURDAY
1
2 3 4 5 6 7 8
9 10 11 12 13 14 15
16 17 18 19 20 21 22
23 24 25 26 27 28 29
30 31

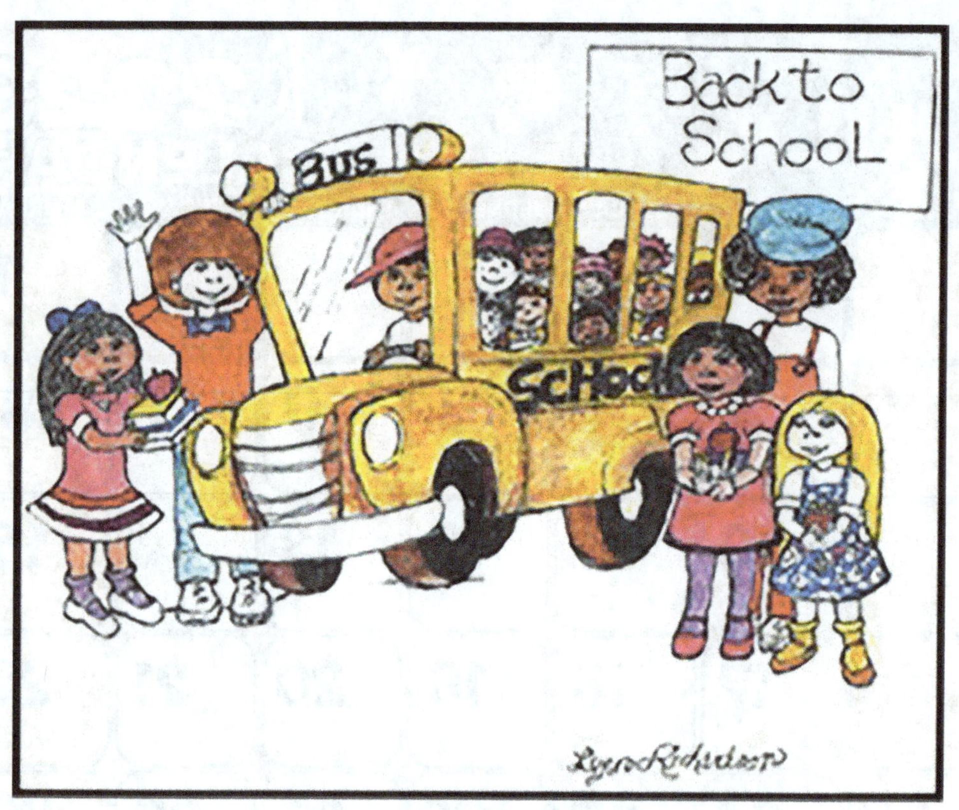

AUGUST

BACK TO SCHOOL MAGIC BUS WORKSHEET

On the first day of school students will get to design their own "Back to School Magic Bus" worksheet. Pictures of school buses will be handed out. Students can draw their own imaginative magic school bus and record important information such as their name and address, name of their school, principal, new teacher, homeroom, etc. Students should record the date they started back and make a list of new friends and old friends that they are glad to see again.

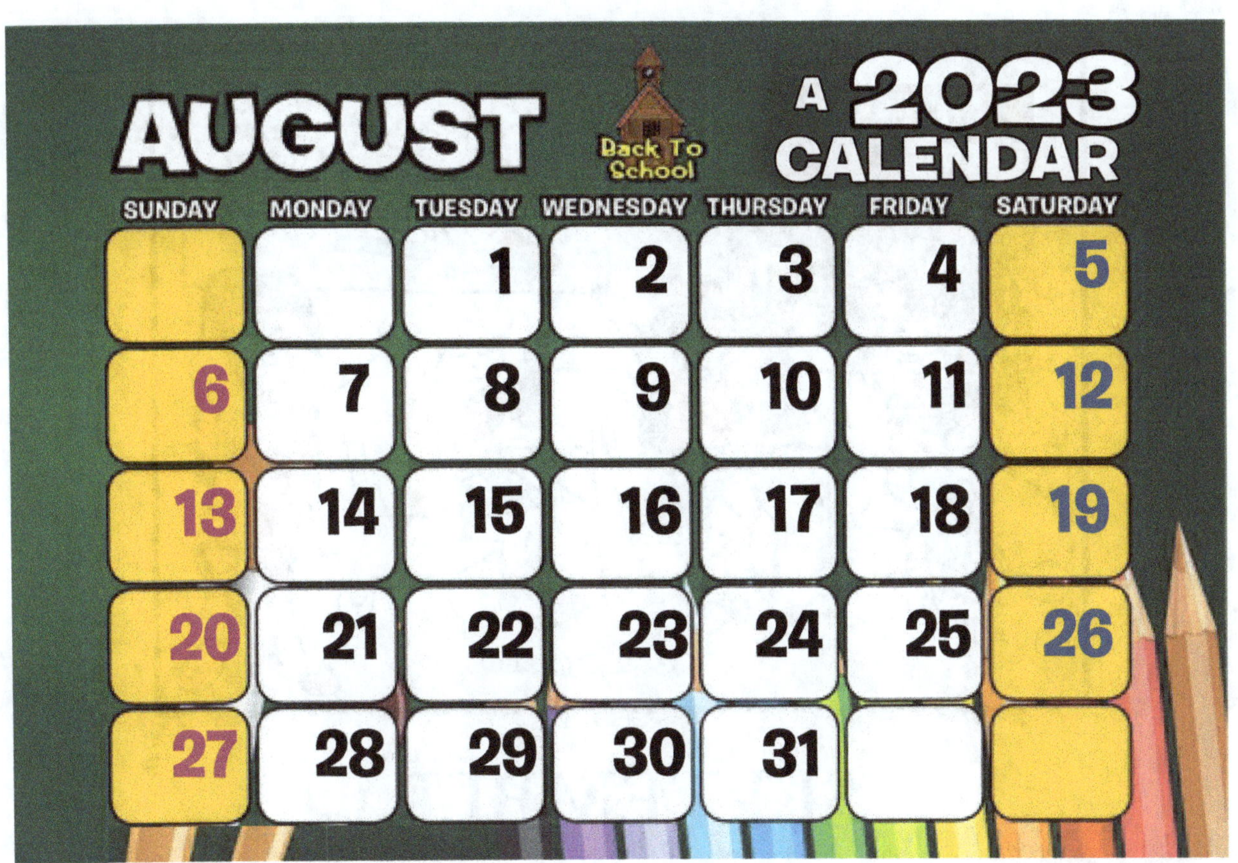

AUGUST
Back To School
A 2023 CALENDAR
SUNDAY
MONDAY
TUESDAY
WEDNESDAY
THURSDAY
FRIDAY
SATURDAY
1
2
3
4
5
6
7
8
9
10
11
12
13
14
15
16
17
18
19
20
21
22
23
24
25
26
27
28
29
30
31

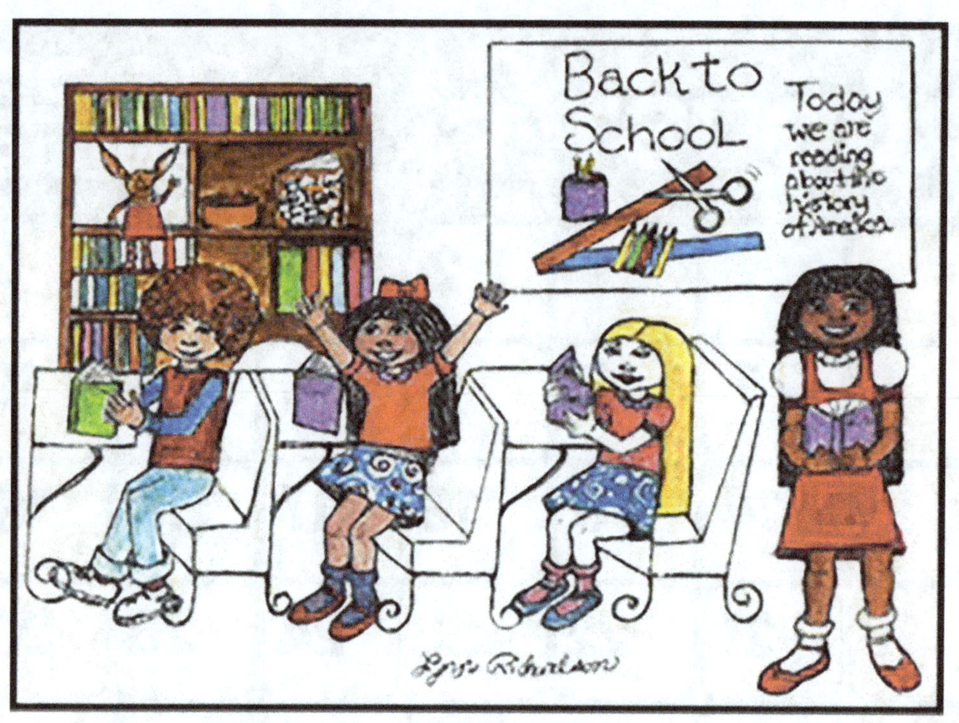

SEPTEMBER

EXPLORING COLONIAL AMERICA

Students will explore what life was like in colonial America. They will engage in popcorn reading and choral reading in books about colonial life and break up into discussion groups of four. Each group will do an oral and written presentation of what interested them the most about colonial life. Underneath their written work, they may draw a picture of themselves and their family members in their own imaginative colonial setting.

SEPTEMBER

A 2023 CALENDAR

SUNDAY	MONDAY	TUESDAY	WEDNESDAY	THURSDAY	FRIDAY	SATURDAY
					1	2
3	4	5	6	7	8	9
10	11	12	13	14	15	16
17	18	19	20	21	22	23
24	25	26	27	28	29	30

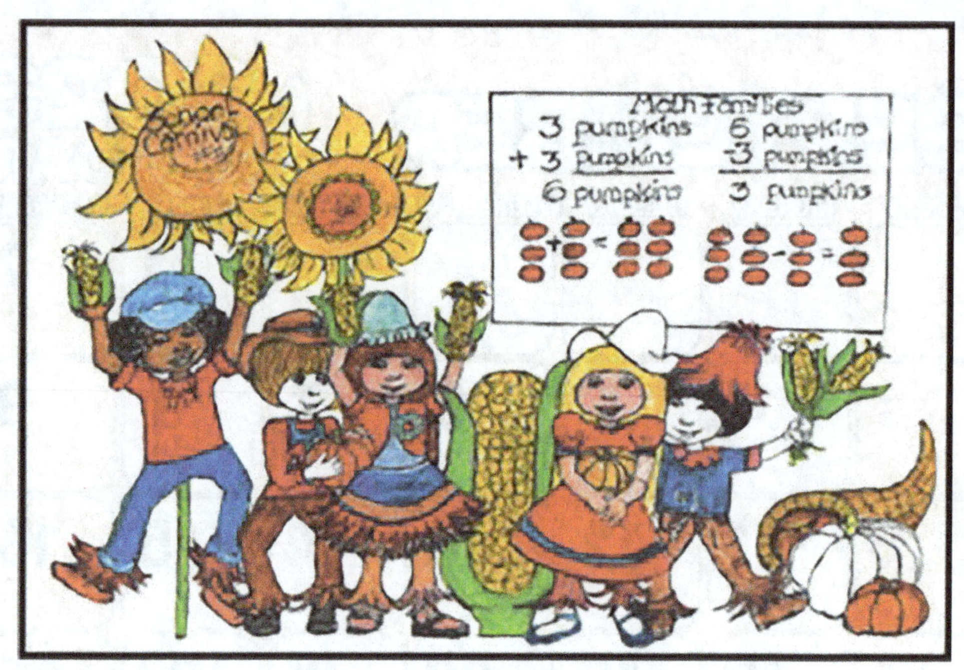

OCTOBER

PUMPKINS, INDIANS, AND CORN HUSK DOLLS

Children will work on solving addition and subtraction problems by using plastic pumpkin counters or candy corn as hands-on learning tools. Students will engage in pair-share reading in stories about pumpkins, Indians, and corn. http://www.teachersfirst.com/ is a website that teachers can use to share with their students on how to make Native American Indian corn husk dolls step by step.

OCTOBER A 2023 CALENDAR

SUNDAY	MONDAY	TUESDAY	WEDNESDAY	THURSDAY	FRIDAY	SATURDAY
1	2	3	4	5	6	7
8	9	10	11	12	13	14
15	16	17	18	19	20	21
22	23	24	25	26	27	28
29	30	31				

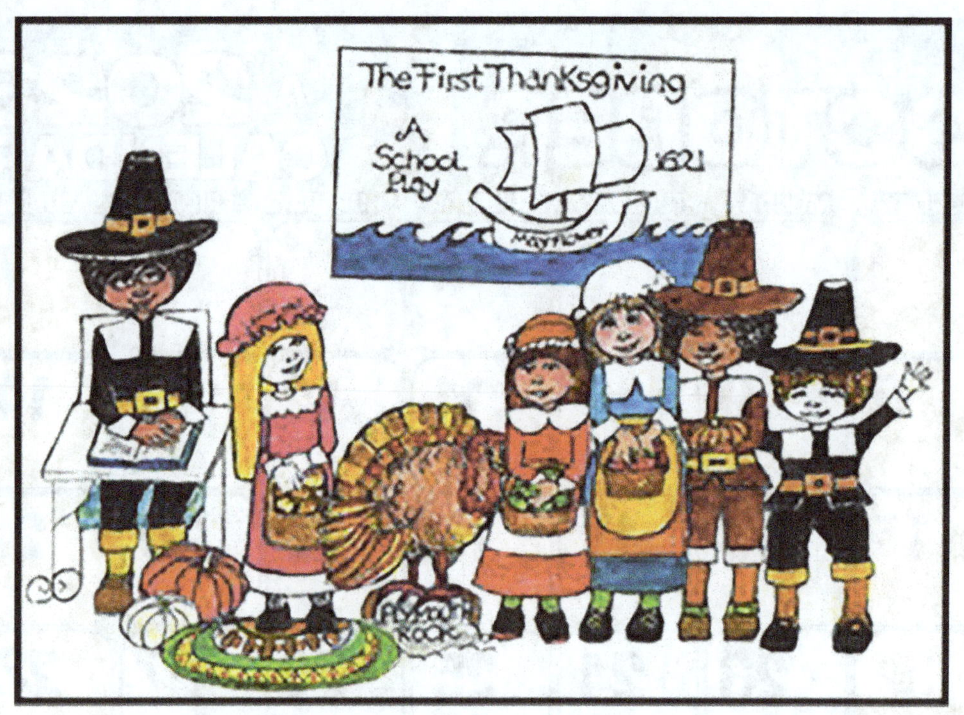

NOVEMBER

THE FIRST THANKSGIVING

Students will read short stories about the first thanksgiving. They will explore how Squanto and the other Native American tribes helped the pilgrims plant corn and showed them how to survive in their new land. The children can engage in a TPR activity (Total Physical Response) by putting on their own version in a re- enactment of the first thanksgiving.

NOVEMBER A 2023 CALENDAR

SUNDAY	MONDAY	TUESDAY	WEDNESDAY	THURSDAY	FRIDAY	SATURDAY
			1	2	3	4
5	6	7	8	9	10	11
12	13	14	15	16	17	18
19	20	21	22	23	24	25
26	27	28	29	30		

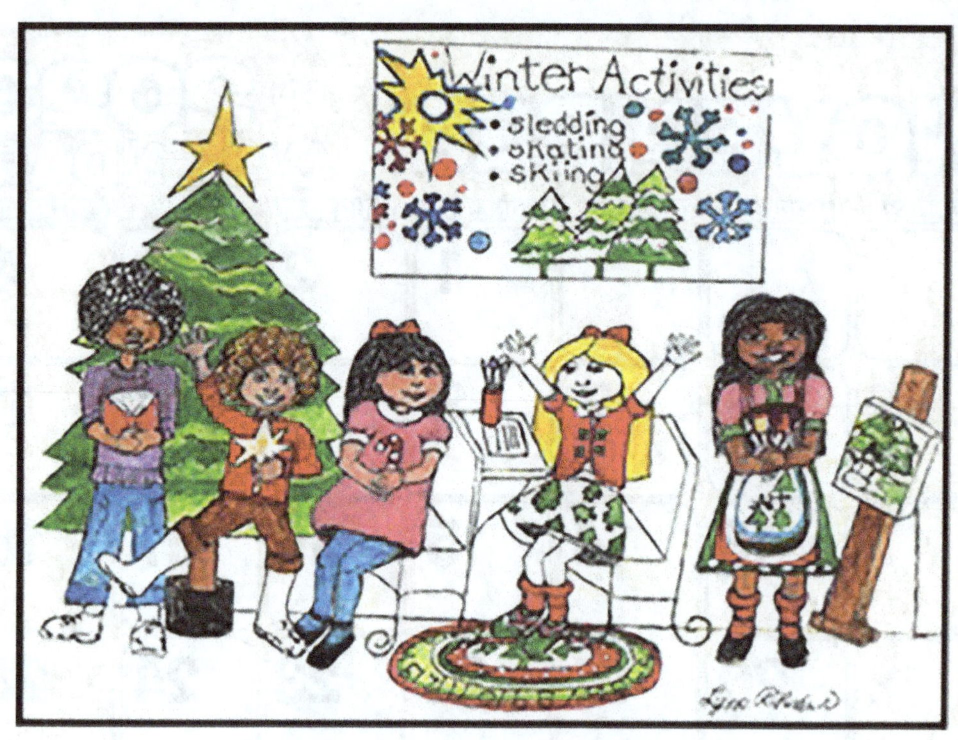

DECEMBER

PAPER SNOWFLAKES AND Q-TIP DESIGNS

Teacher gives handouts on the winter season and snowflake formation. Students can create unique snowflake designs by drawing and tracing various snowflake patterns onto white paper. Students may cut them out and paste them onto different colored construction papers or glue them onto wooden craft sticks. For variety, students can collect Q-tips and form them into snowflake patterns. They can glue them onto construction paper. Children may listen to songs on CD's about winter activities. After they write their descriptive sentences about winter and snowflakes, students can place and paste them underneath their designs.

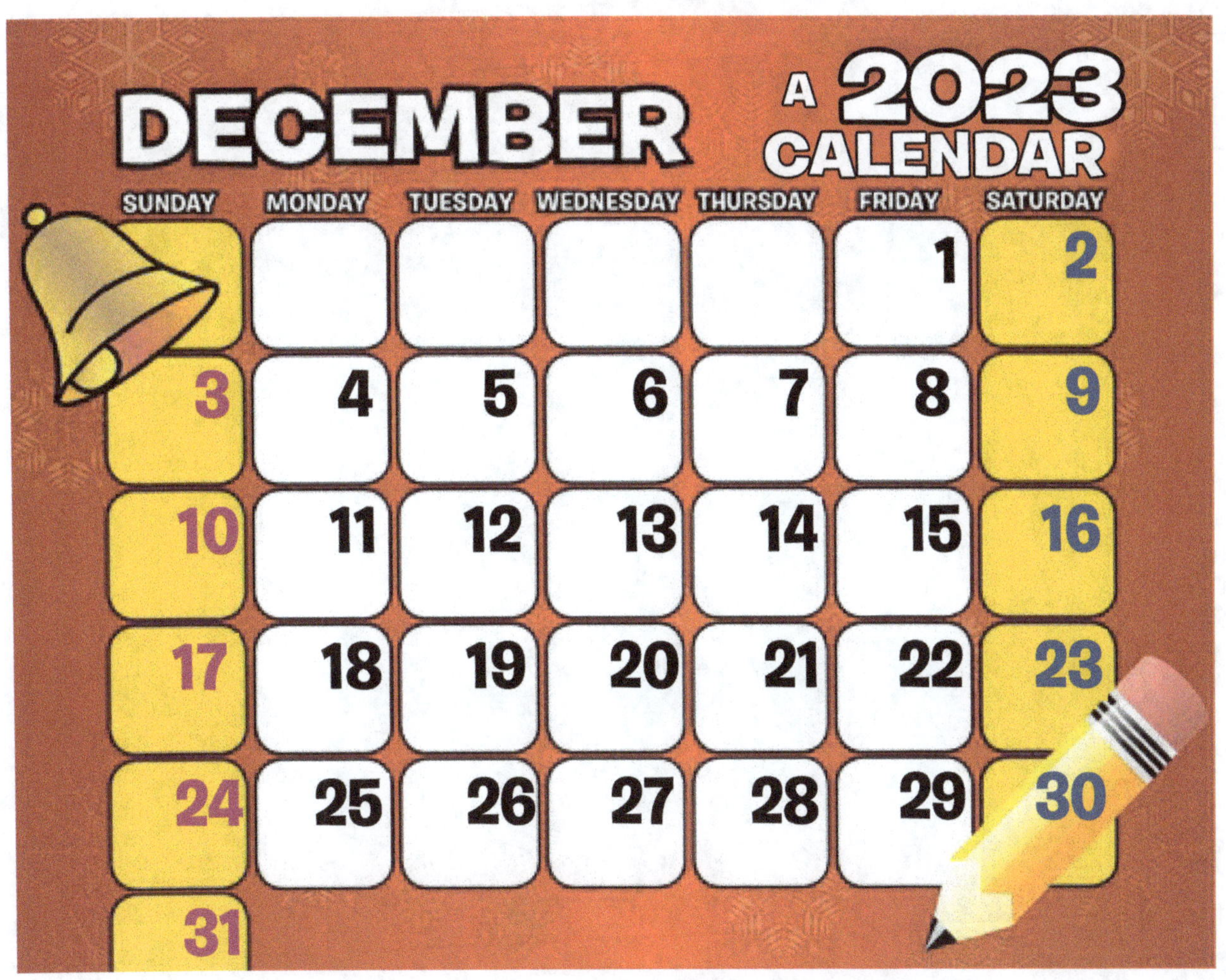

DECEMBER
A 2023 CALENDAR
SUNDAY MONDAY TUESDAY WEDNESDAY THURSDAY FRIDAY SATURDAY
1 2
3 4 5 6 7 8 9
10 11 12 13 14 15 16
17 18 19 20 21 22 23
24 25 26 27 28 29 30
31